LET'S BELIEVE

LET'S BELIEVE

by Agnes Sanford

Illustrations by Ted Sanford

Religious Book Department
HARPER & BROTHERS PUBLISHERS
New York

Library of Congress catalogue card number: 54-5854

TO TED AND ANDY
This book is lovingly dedicated

LET'S BELIEVE

Chapter One

><<

RIGHT-SIDE-UP

Right-side-up I'm a fairy queen,
    But up-side-down I'm a pest.
Up-side-down I am frightfully mean!
    It's right-side-up I am best.

Right-side-up you're a storybook knight,
    But up-side-down you're a knave.
Up-side-down you're a pitiful sight!
    And right-side-up you are brave.

Look at the funny faces on this page. They seem happy, don't they? You smile when you see them. But now turn the book up-side-down. Where have all the happy faces gone? The smiling queen has turned into a mean woman and she isn't happy at all. The knight isn't a knight any more, he is an ugly, angry man. The funny fellow in the tiny cap looks the way you feel on the days when everything goes wrong. If you stared very long at all these sad faces you'd start feeling unhappy yourself. So turn the book right-side-up again. There they are, the smiling queen and the brave knight and the smiling little boy and girl.

All the right-side-up people are happy and all the up-side-down people are unhappy and they change very fast.

That is just the way it is with you and me. Some days we feel fine and everything is nice. Breakfast tastes good and Skippy makes us laugh when he teases Bingo, the yellow cat. We skip to school and it is fun, and then we run and race and laugh out in the sun and think of lovely games to play. Even after we go to bed we watch the light through the cracks of the door and hear

Mother's voice in the living-room and think happy thoughts about tomorrow.

But sometimes the world seems up-side-down and Mother says, "Did you get out of the wrong side of the bed today?"

We did not get out of the wrong side of the bed and that is a silly question anyway, because one side of the bed is the same as another. But we don't feel like ourselves and we might as well be upside down. We feel cross. If somebody says "Yes" we feel like saying "No." When they say "It isn't" we want to shout " 'Tis too!" Breakfast is horrid and Bingo yells when we pull his tail and Skippy runs away and will not play with us. Everybody at school is mean. And when we get home, we can't think of anything that is fun to do and we lie on the floor and look at the television and that isn't fun either.

Sometimes we feel that way because we are getting sick. And sometimes we don't know why we feel that way—we just do.

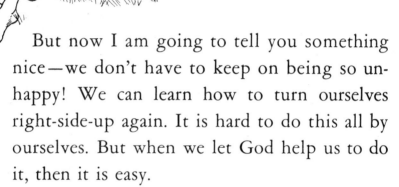

But now I am going to tell you something nice—we don't have to keep on being so unhappy! We can learn how to turn ourselves right-side-up again. It is hard to do this all by ourselves. But when we let God help us to do it, then it is easy.

You see, it is like this—God made us, and so I think He likes us to be well and to be good, don't you? When you make anything, you like it to be good. If you draw a paper doll, you try to make it as nice a doll as you can. When you build a snow fort, you build one as big and strong as any one can build. It is no fun to make things unless you try to make them good. Even when you were younger and played with blocks, you wanted to build fine houses out of them. Sometimes you tried but you couldn't, because you were not smart enough. Sometimes you tried, but other people came along and knocked them down. You did not like that, because you really wanted them to be good.

God is able to make us well and strong and happy all the time. But sometimes mean things come along and spoil what God has made. I don't think God likes this, because I notice that if we give Him a chance, He will always help us to be right-side-up again. He tries to do it even without our asking. He has made our bodies so that they are always mending themselves. But He can help us much better if we will play a believing game with Him. Most games are better when at least two people play. Sometimes you try to play ball alone, throwing it against the wall and catching it when it comes back. But you can do it much better if someone plays with you.

So in this book we are going to learn how to play a game with God. I call it the believing game.

MIDSUMMER

God's light is on the meadows,
   He's talking to the trees,
He's smiling on the butterflies
   And on the honeybees.

What fun it is to laugh with Him
   At bright and dancing things—
At hummingbirds and dragonflies
   With shining, silver wings!

When I am mad and all upset,
   Even the sunlight's dim,
So when I want to fuss and fret
   I'll stop and think of Him.

Chapter Two

꘍꘍꘍❌꘍꘍꘍

WIND IN MY HAIR

Wind in my hair blows low, blows low,
   Wind in my hair blows high,
Wind in my hair blows dancing snow
   Out of a dancing sky.

Wind in my skirts makes me scamper and race,
   Wind in my eyes makes me cry,
But wind will not show me his blustering face—
   Sometimes I do wonder why.

   Of course the wind can't show us his face. He hasn't any face. He hasn't any arms or legs or anything. And yet there is a wind. We know there is, because we can feel it and we can see the

things that happen when the wind blows. We can see yellow leaves fly high in the sky like shiny birds and come to rest again, all whispering and crisp. We can see the trees bend their heads and sunflowers dance a golden dance in the sunlight. We know the wind is blowing.

In a way God is like the wind. He hasn't any face or arms or legs either. He does not need a body to live in, because He lives in everything. He is in the air and the sunlight and the wind and He is outside them too, just living, all by Himself, in a way so big that we cannot quite imagine it. But we know there is a God because we feel different when He comes inside of us and turns us right-side-up again. And we know there is a God because we see other things that He does. He makes the sun come up in the morning and the flowers bloom in the spring.

All the things that God makes try very hard to grow up in just the right way. If a crocus is trying to push its way out of a pile of dead leaves, it gets very tired of working so hard and it is thin and pale. But if you move the leaves away, it will hurry like anything to catch up with the other flowers and be just as beautiful as it can be.

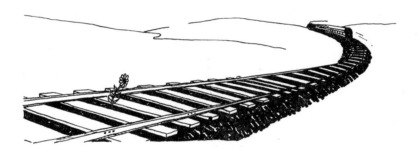

Once when I was traveling in Florida I saw a tiny purple flower growing in the gravel between the ties on the railway track, and I thought, "If we tried as hard as that flower does to use every bit of God's earth and sunshine, how wonderful we would be!"

How can we grow the way God meant us to grow?

First of all, we can call God and listen until we feel that He is near us.

When I was a little girl in China there were no trains or planes or automobiles and we would travel in a houseboat. We played and ate and slept on our houseboat. Our boat had sails and when there was a good wind the boatmen used the sails and our boat would move right along the canal. But when there was no wind, the Chinese boatmen would use long poles to push the boat through the brown water of the canal, bending low and groaning as they pushed. They got very tired of this pushing. So then they would stand up straight and wipe their hot faces and look far away and call the wind. "Ooo —loo—loo—loo—" they would say. And they would watch and listen and then they would call again. "Ooo—loo—loo—loo—." I do not know whether their calling really brought the wind or not. When I was a little girl, I used to think that it did. For often the wind would begin to blow and the sails would fill and the houseboat would move through the dark water,

slowly, slowly, creak, creak, in the tired way that houseboats move.

The wind does not always blow stronger when we call to it. But when we call to God, His power always grows stronger in us. God is everywhere, as the wind is everywhere. There can be so little wind that you do not feel it at all, or there can be so much wind that it pushes you along and you have to run to keep up with it. And there can be so little of God in you that you feel empty or there can be so much of Him that your unhappy feelings go flying out of your mind and the happy feelings come back.

So let's try calling God. Be quiet now and shut your eyes, because it is easier to think of God when you are not looking at outside things. Then say, "God, please come and blow away all my unhappy feelings. Please come and shine in me like the sunlight and make me feel good again."

There is a special name for talking to God. It is called prayer. But prayer is more than talking. It is also listening for God's answer. He always answers if we truly want Him to answer.

Chapter Three

※

GOD HAS A LIGHT

I turn on the light and how quickly it shines!
    When I turn on the water it flows.
I turn on the fan and it whiffles around,
    While the cool wind blows and blows.

If I don't turn the knob, then I don't have a light;
    If I don't turn the tap, it is dry.
If I don't turn the fan it is perfectly still—
    It is not at all hard to see why!

The light is not gone, it is waiting for me,
    The water is ready to flow,
And if only I know how to turn on the fan,
    It is perfectly willing to go.

God gave me all of these wonderful things,
   And is waiting to give me some more,
For God has a way He can fill me with life,
   If I learn how to open the door.

It would be foolish, wouldn't it, if you stood in front of your electric fan without pushing the switch and said over and over, "Fan, please blow."

And what a goose you would be if you said, "I don't believe in electric lights because I asked this light to shine and it isn't shining."

Of course it isn't shining when you did not turn it on! Just asking it is not enough to make it shine.

Suppose you were thirsty and you ran into the kitchen and stood before the sink and said, "Come on, water, flow into this glass!"—and did not turn on the faucet.

You would not want your older brother to see you standing there like that.

"What do you think you're doing?" he would laugh.

And suppose you said, "Well, I just don't believe the water *wants* to flow into this glass"—and you still did not turn it on.

How he would tease you for being so foolish!

Yet people pray that way all the time. Even grown people forget that just asking for God's power is not enough. They must turn it on too. The reason we must turn it on is that God's power is *real,* like wind and water. When He sends His power into us and makes us feel good again, He is not doing a magic trick. He is giving us something as real as electric light. His power brightens up everything in us just as electric light brightens up everything in a room.

When Jesus came into the world to show us what God is like, He told His friends about this real, real power. People did not know about electricity then, or about radio, or about television. So it was hard to explain to them that there could be a light that you cannot see or a sound that you cannot hear. Nowadays we know that this is so. We cannot see the light that comes into the aerial outside of the house. But

when we turn on the television set, then we can see it, making a bright picture for us. So we know that it is real. We cannot hear Hopalong Cassidy until we turn on the radio. Then we can hear him. So we know that his voice is there in the air, just waiting for us to turn it on.

Jesus had a hard time explaining to His friends that there is more in the world than they were able to see. Some day, He told them, they would understand God's power much better. But Jesus tried in every way He could to make them know that this power is real and that it works in a real way. He called it the water of life—and we turn it on as we turn on water. He called it the light of the world—and we turn it on as we turn on light. He called it the breath or the

Spirit of God—and we turn it on as we turn on the breath of the electric fan.

Now how can we turn it on? Jesus told us that too. He said that when we prayed for something, we must believe that it is happening. It is our believing which turns on the power.

But how can we believe in the power when we cannot see whether it is coming or not?

Here is the way I teach myself to believe it is coming—I play a pretend-game about it. When I call God and ask Him for something, I pretend that it is happening, and then I say, "Thank You, God, You are helping me right now." After I say this for a while, I begin to feel that He is really doing it, and then the pretend-game changes to a believing game. And before long, the thing that I prayed for is very likely to happen.

Why do you suppose God wants us to believe?

He isn't just a Great, Big Meany sitting up in the sky, thinking "I'm not going to make Jimmy well until he believes I will." He simply cannot answer our prayers unless we believe. We are made that way. Inside of us there is a little mind that runs the body. It is a different mind from the mind that thinks. It saves our thinking mind so much trouble because it can work while we sleep or play or read or eat. It keeps our body machinery running. We don't have to sit down and think about how food is going to make blood and bones and hair for us. The little mind inside, which I call Junior, takes care of all of that. Junior is very clever. When we cut our fingers, Junior mends them. When we breathe in the little germs that make us sick, Junior calls out the blood cells to kill them before they have time to bother us. But sometimes Junior cannot work so well. He seems to get tired or mad and give up. Why? Maybe he thinks, "What's the use of trying to get Jimmy well when he will only stuff himself again with things that make him sick?" Or maybe he says, "There are so many of these germs flying around that I can't fight them all by myself."

Junior is very clever, but he does get con-

fused. We have to speak plainly to him. If he is working to make us well and we say "I feel very sick!" he listens to our main word "sick." So he thinks, "Oh, he wants to be sick." Then he does not know what to do. He feels our discouraged feelings and says to himself, "Oh dear, I just can't manage all these germs."

But if we say, "Thank You, God, You are making me well," then Junior begins to get the idea, especially if we say over and over, "Thank You, God."

After a while Junior thinks, "Say! I'd better get going again and make this fellow well! God's in here helping me, and with Him I can really do it!"

So that is why God wants us to believe. It is on account of the way we are made.

T.V.

The picture that shines in the bright T.V.
   Is made of a light that I cannot see,
As it comes in the aerial, high in the sky,
    Out of the night where the moon rides by.
     It's awfully odd, but it's so, you know,
      It's awfully odd,
       But it's so.

For God can make anything—darkness and light,
   The woods and the fields and stars in the night,
Mountains so tall that they scrape the skies
   And dear little kittens with shining eyes—
    And I'm awfully glad that it's so, you know,
    I'm awfully glad
     That it's so.

Chapter Four

SEASIDE

I'll shut my eyes and pretend I can be
  Down by the side of the thundering sea,
Where the sea gulls wheel on their great white
    wings,
  And the wind shouts loud and the blown sand
    sings.

Thank You, Lord, that I'll soon be there,
  Sand in my toes and wind in my hair,
While the sun burns hot in the high blue sky
  And the big white clouds go marching by.

The next time you get sick, say "Thank You, God, that You are making me well" over and over again so that Junior gets the idea. Then you must talk nicely to Junior, because that little mind has to be cheered up as it goes along. So you can say, "Thanks, Junior, you're doing a good job in there."

There are some other games that you can play with Junior. Do you know that your body is made up of lots of little cells? They are so small that you can't see them, but if you could see them, they would look like tiny soap bubbles. All of these cells can hear you when you talk to them. So if you like you can help Junior in his work by giving them a pep talk. You can play that these cells are soldiers and you are their captain, just as you may play that chessmen are soldiers and you are their captain. Maybe you take them into the bathtub with you when you take a bath and pretend you are their captain and push them around as they float beside the soap. So you can play that the cells in your body are soldiers and you are the commanding officer. And you can say, "Look here, you fellows, I'd like to know who's boss inside of me. So now you listen, and do just what I say."

U. S. 857322

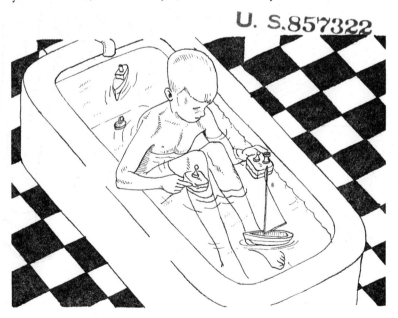

Then I play that they are all hurrying around killing germs, and I say, "Good! That's fine! Pretty soon you'll have me well."

And I don't forget to say, "Thank You, God, for helping them make me well."

When the doctor comes to see me, I say "Thank You" for him too. Because he is my friend and he is God's helper and he gives me extra cell food that we call medicine.

Then I play the believing game again. I shut my eyes and play that I am out in the sun running around and feeling wonderful. I plan what I will do as soon as I get out-of-doors. And pretty soon I begin to feel happier and stronger.

If I get awfully hot for a while as I am thinking this way, I know that those cells are hurrying up like everything. So I say to myself, "This fever is a good idea right now. My body is using it to burn out germs. And as soon as it has done what it is trying to do, it will go away."

Then I shut my eyes again and think of the very nicest place in all of the great big out-of-doors, the place where I'd like best to be if I

could choose out of all the places in the world.
And I say, "Thank You, God, for I'll be out
doors playing very soon."

Chapter Five

SHINING WORLD

Silver wings in a silver sky
And a shining plane goes flying by!

Silver wings on a silver sea
And a sea gull flutters his tail at me,

He flutters his tail and he winks his eye
And I think he laughs as he sails on by.

So many wonderful things in the sky,
From a shining plane to a dragon fly!

So many wonderful things to see,
From a big balloon to a bumblebee!

I must really remember, every day
To thank the Lord for a world so gay.

Being sick is not the only thing that gets us up-side-down. Sometimes we are up-side-down because Dad and Mother are cross or because Dad is worried about his business or because Mother is upset over the baby's teething. It takes more of God's power to make us happy if the trouble is something like this, because then God has to help two or three people instead of just one and they may not all believe He can help them. But He can still do it if we will believe He can. And we can try believing about Dad and Mother just as we have learned to believe about ourselves. We can make a picture in our minds of Mother smiling again and of Dad whistling as he comes into the front door. Then we can say, "Thank You, God, Your light is shining into Mother and Dad and making them happy."

We can even think about Dad's business and say, "Thank You, God, I know You will help Dad with his work. You worked to make the whole world, and you work to keep it going. So of course You can help Dad to work."

We can ask God to help Mother take care of the baby too, and maybe we can help her a little ourselves. We can also make a picture in our minds of Mother smiling.

Now what is it that makes her smile when we have not said anything but we are only seeing a picture in our minds?

It is God's power that we have helped to turn on. We have turned on God's light just as we turn on the light in the television set, making the picture come alive. We are getting God's program of good feeling inside of us and sending it out to somebody else. Maybe

that was what Jesus meant when He said we
should be like a light. In fact, He even said
that we *are* a kind of light. And He said that
we should not hide that light under a bushel
basket, but we should let it shine out.

Have you ever stood on your front steps on
a summer night in the country and watched the
fireflies making little bright places in the grass?
There wouldn't be any lights in the grass if the
fireflies all hid under a basket. But they would
not want to hide. They have fun flying around
and flashing their little lights. And we can have
even more fun with this different kind of a
light that God has put in us.

Chapter Six

꧁꧂

NIGHT TRAIN

The train has a clackety, clackety song,
  The train says clackety, clack,
And all of the houses go rushing along,
  Out of the night so black.

But after the journey is over at last
  The houses are still as can be.
What made them seem to be flying past?
  Was it only the train and me?

That's true, you know, about trains.

Your eyes tell you that houses and trees are rushing beside the train, and they are not really moving at all. Did you ever stand on the back platform of a train? Your eyes tell you that the track is getting smaller and the shining lines of rails are swinging closer together. But your eyes are not telling the truth, for the railroad tracks are really just the same.

So when you try believing, do not pay too much attention to what your eyes tell you or to what your feelings tell you. Do not look at yourself and say, "God isn't sending His light into me. I feel just the same."

Maybe one day you feel sick. Your mother says you are sick. The doctor says you are sick. But you do not want to be sick. You intend to get well quickly. So you ask God to make you strong and happy the way He intended you to be. You play the believing game. Minutes go by and you don't feel any better. Does that mean that you are not really getting better?

Oh no!

I know a beech tree, its trunk smooth and gray, its branches stretching out, way out, low over the ground. In April when the winds begin whispering about spring, the ground is bare and brown under it where the snow used to be. My eyes tell me that there are no flowers there. But there are! The prettiest flowers in the world are there—gold and purple crocuses and tiny blue scyllas, bluer than the sky, bluer than the sea, bluer than anything. They are growing under the ground, even though my eyes do not see them.

Then the spring days go by and all the blue scyllas come popping and shining up. And there

is the beech tree, with flowers like a carpet all over the ground beneath it and its branches low and twisty reaching out over them with dewdrops shining on their tiny leaf buds. It is so pretty that you can almost see the fairies playing there. It is so pretty that you want to dance and laugh when you see it, and even to think of it in the night makes you smile in the happy dark.

They were there all the time, getting ready to pop out, even when you could see nothing but snow.

That is the way health is inside of you. It is waiting to bloom, and when you believe, then God's power is making it stronger so that soon you will know you are well.

LITTLE BLUE FLOWER

Little blue flower, you're very sweet
When spring comes dancing on silver feet
  And the robins cry
    In the high blue sky
That winter has gone with its snow and its sleet.

I used to be sad when you withered away
From under the beech where the fairies play,
  But now I know
    That you never do go,
You're right in the ground, and another fine day

When spring comes glimmering over the hill
And the polliwogs peep in the brook by the mill,
  You'll open your eyes
    And smile at the skies
And laugh as you tell me you're here with me still.

Chapter Seven

꧁⸙꧂

VEGETABLES

God gives us red tomatoes,
 And peas within a pod.
Tomatoes, peas and radishes
 Have all been made by God.

BUT—

Tomatoes can't grow radishes,
 Or peas within a pod,
Tomatoes can't grow scrambled eggs—
 That's not the plan of God!

Now you will tell me, "Don't be silly."

But some people are just as silly as that when it comes to prayer. They pray for things that are foolish and when you ask them why, they say, "Because all things are possible with God."

Of course all things are possible with Him. He could do foolish things if He wanted to do them, but He doesn't, because He isn't foolish.

Once when I was a very, very little girl, I prayed that when I woke up in the morning I would see a drum and a doll growing on a bush outside of the window. Some grown person had told me that all things are possible with God and forgot to tell me that God does not do foolish things, so I asked Him to grow a doll and drum on a bush.

I am glad you are not so foolish. You know that you could not pray for your tomato plants to grow radishes or peas.

Could you pray for your tomato plants to have better tomatoes? Certainly you could! And God's rain and sun would help them to be good tomatoes and your love would help them too. So you and God together could grow lovely tomatoes. But you could pray all day long and all night long for the tomato plants to grow radishes and no radishes would grow.

If you had blue eyes and you thought brown eyes were prettier, could you ask God to change blue eyes into brown eyes? No. That would be foolishness. God does not do things like that. But if you were not a pretty little girl and it made you feel unhappy when people said, "Isn't it too bad that her brother has all the looks of the family?" could you ask God to make you prettier? Certainly you could! That is not foolish, that is sensible! God must like pretty things, it seems to me, or He would not have made little tiny flowers and great big flowers all different and all lovely, and painted clouds at sunset-time and silver dewdrops in the morning. God can make you grow prettier in ways of His own. He can give you shining eyes and a merry smile and a gay heart and everyone will say, "Isn't she lovely!" And as you grow older even your nose and mouth can grow into prettier lines.

SILLY THINGS

I wouldn't pray for a horse with horns
    Or a dog with a light on his tail,
I wouldn't ask to jump over the moon
    Or to go out to sea on a whale!

I wouldn't pray for my skin to be blue
    Or my hair to be green as the sod,
For I wouldn't be silly—and neither would you—
    And neither, I think, would God.

Chapter Eight

❧

TO AN AIRPLANE

You're as heavy, as heavy, as heavy as lead,
    And yet you're so light you can fly,
Soaring and roaring up over my head
    And high in the summery sky!

All the king's horses and all the king's men
    Couldn't lift you away from the ground,
Yet there you go roaring and soaring again,
    With a frightfully frightening sound.

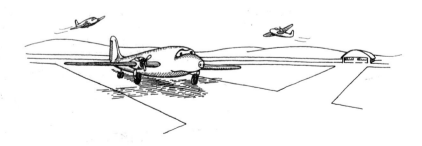

Men made you heavy, yet men made you fly
  On shimmering, silvery wings ,
And if men can do that, then I do not see why
  They should wonder at heavenly things!

Nobody would say, "Why does an airplane have to have wings? Why does it have to have an engine?"

But people are always expecting God to do things which make no more sense than asking a plane to fly without an engine. They will say, "If God wants somebody to be well, why doesn't He just make them well? Why does He care whether anybody prays and how they pray and whether they believe what they say?"

Now of course God makes many people well all the time whether they pray or whether they don't. He has made our bodies so that they mend cuts and kill germs and do wonderful things to keep us well. And He has provided the good medicines that doctors use when our bodies need help in healing us. But sometimes we need even more help than this, and we believe that He has an extra power that can come into us.

But that power works by law just as an airplane works by law, and to expect God to send His extra power into us when we have not prepared a way for it is just as big a mistake as expecting an airplane to fly without wings and without an engine. Prayer is the engine for His power. And the wings are made by believing. The wings and the engine have to be in good repair or they will not work, just as an airplane cannot fly if its wings and its engine are broken.

And I do not think you will be so foolish as to ask Him why. You would be like a fellow playing baseball who said to the coach, "But I don't see why the ball has to go inside of first base. Why can't it go just anywhere?"

The coach would say, "Listen, Bud. Those are the rules. Either you play ball or you don't play ball, see. But if you play ball, those are the rules."

It is the same way with God's power. Either you play the believing game or you don't play it, but if you play it, there are some rules.

God's rules are called laws. Some people call them the laws of nature. If you put your hand in the fire, it will burn you. That is a law of nature. There is no use in saying, "Why does God let it burn?" That is God's business. He needs fire and He has made it. And He has given you enough sense to obey the law of fire.

If you jump in deep water, you will drown. That is a law. But if you learn to swim, then you can jump into deep water and not drown. That is another law. It does not mean that God has broken His laws when you learn to swim. It means that you have learned to use other laws of God. You cannot walk across the ocean to China. But if you get in a ship, you can go across that same ocean to China. That is another law.

If you step off a cliff, you may get killed. But if you have a parachute and jump off a cliff, you will not get killed. You have hold of something that lifts you above the force called gravity that makes people fall down.

A train cannot run in the sky. That is a law. But if men build a trestle—a track on high poles—then it can run high above your head. That is another law.

All this I have said before but I am saying it over again because it is so very important for people to understand that God does things in sensible ways and not by magic. If we do not get the answers to all our prayers, it may not be because God does not want to give them to us. It may be because we have not learned the laws through which He has to work. But the more we try to pray in the right way, the more we learn. So we work away at our believing wings and we do not give up if sometimes they seem to fly and sometimes they do not. They will get better and stronger as we grow up. And they will have more power as more people learn to pray, until the whole world is filled with God's power.

ELEVATED RAILWAY

What a funny thing 'twould be
To see a train climb up a tree,

To see a train go rattling by
Out of the night up in the sky!

Yet away in the city, so I've heard,
There's a train that can fly as high as a bird,

For people have made it an upstairs track,
With steps that go up and steps that come back.

Now isn't that funny and isn't that odd?
But people are clever, and so is God.

Chapter Nine

->>)<<-

WATER

Water will not flow uphill,
　　It simply cannot be.
It ripples down a little rill
And on to rivers deep and still,
　　Because of gravity.

For God has got a set of rules
　　By which His world is made,
And wind and water, birds and mules,
And people, if they are not fools,
　　Will do what He has said.

Did you ever try to make water flow uphill?
If it is a good day and Mother doesn't mind,
why don't you go out-of-doors right now and
dig a tiny ditch on a sloping place and a hole
at the bottom of your ditch, and then pour some
water down the ditch and see which way it flows.
Will it flow downhill into the hole or will it
flow uphill or will it flow out to the sides? It
will flow downhill of course. That is because

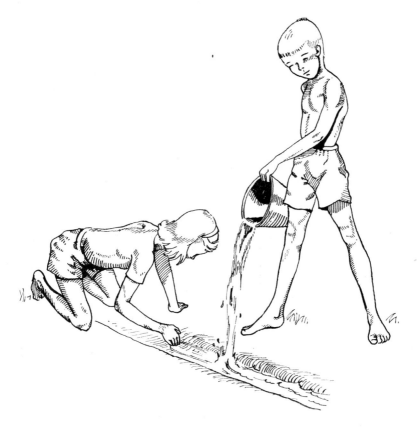

of a force called gravity which pulls everything toward the earth. If it were not for the earth's gravity, when you throw a ball into the air it would never come back. Gravity is one of God's laws and it cannot be broken.

Now take some stones and some dirt and build a dam across your ditch and pour some water down it as you did before, and see where the water will go. Maybe a little will still trickle into the hole, but most of it will flow out to the sides above your dam.

There! We said it had to go down into the hole because of the law of gravity. What has happened? Have we broken the law of gravity?

Of course not! We put something in the way, that's all.

Now if you are praying for a sensible thing like getting well or like being able to learn your arithmetic and if you really believe that God is helping you, then God's extra power is bound to come into you. That is a law, just like the law of gravity. It is the law of prayer, and nothing can break that law. But sometimes you pray for these sensible things and nothing happens. You keep on believing and you give it time to happen and still nothing happens. Well then, what is the trouble? Is the law of prayer refusing to work?

No, of course not. The trouble must be that you have put something in the way of God. But you have dug a believing ditch for God's power! Well then, what is big enough to stop that power from coming in?

Hate can stop His power, because God is love. And being mean to people can stop it. Hate and meanness make a dam in your mind, as the stones and dirt made a dam in your ditch. God's love meets that dam in your mind and it cannot get through. Or maybe a little bit trickles through, as a little bit of water works its way through your dam of stones and dirt. Because God's love is very strong, just as the force of gravity is very strong. He seems to try hard to reach us with His love. So that you may get a little bit of God's power in spite of all the dams inside of you. But if you want more of it, so that you can get right-side-up in a faster, happier way, the next thing to do is to move those stones out of the way.

How can you do that?

It is easy to try.

If you are sick and feel fussy you can smile at Mother and say, "Thanks!" when she brings your lunch tray instead of growling and fussing and saying, "No! I don't like that! I don't like anything! I want to get up!"

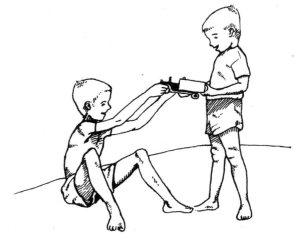

You can let your little brother play with your erector set once in a while instead of always saying, "Give me that! You can't play with my toys!"

Do you see what I mean? Of course you can act in a loving way instead of a mean way if you really want to!

But what if you don't want to be nice? What if you want to fuss and be hateful and ugly and selfish? Well, then the believing game will not work, that is all. Because you are not keeping the law of love. Since God is love, you have to act in a loving way if you want to have God's company. That is the way the game is played. And as the umpire would say in baseball—either you play the game or you don't, but if you do, why—that is the way the game is played.

As I said before, God does not make up His rules just to be mean. Even the rules of baseball are not made to spoil the game, but to help the game, and so are God's rules. Everything goes better for us if we keep them.

But it is not easy to be pleasant and cheerful when we feel like being mean and fussy. It is hard, but that is all the more reason why we should say nice things and think cheerful thoughts even when we do not feel like it. We must learn to be brave if we are going to get along with other people in this world. If you think about it a minute, you will see that this is so. The heroes that you like to read about in the funnies and to see on television are all brave men. You don't like sissies. Nobody likes people who whine and fuss all the time. That is why such people are apt to be lonesome and unhappy. When we learn to say cheerful things and to think loving thoughts even when we are sick, we are learning to grow up brave and strong and all of our lives we will be happier for learning this.

Chapter Ten

✦➤➤❯❮❮✦

TO A FIERCE DOG

God made you and God made me,
  We should be friends, now don't you see?
I like you, so please like me—
  And then what fun our lives will be!

But what if some people are so mean and
horrid that we just can't help hating them and
getting mad when we are with them?

There are ways to keep from hating them,
and we had better learn those ways if we want
to keep right-side-up.

I know a little boy who learned how to be
friends with a dog. Most dogs are nice to chil-

dren, but this was a rude, fierce dog and he didn't like little boys who ride bicycles. So when Tommy rode past his house he would come rushing out and try to knock the bicycle over. Tommy was frightened. When people get frightened, they usually get angry, so Tommy got angry too, and after a while he hated that dog. But he was learning the rules of being right-side-up, as you are learning them. So the next time he rode

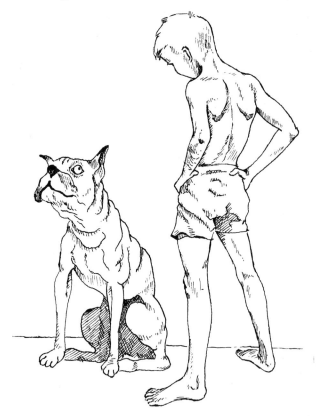

past that dog, he stopped and smiled and said, "God made you and God made me so we ought to be friends. I like you all right, and I think you are going to like me pretty soon." And the dog stopped barking and wagged his tail and they were friends from that time on.

Sometimes it does not work so fast. It may take two or three days and you must be very sure you mean what you say. But if everybody would learn this way of changing mean creatures into friendly creatures, what a wonderful world we would have! After a while maybe grown people would know how to change other grown people, and maybe all the grown people would be so helpful to each other that we would not have wars any more.

There was a little girl named Sally in the fourth grade who did not like the girl in front of her. She said to her mother, "She's horrid! She sticks her fingers in the ink and puts them on my dress and she pulls my hair and she's all dirty and I just can't stand her anyway."

Sally's mother was learning how to make unkind people friendly, so she said to Sally ,"Why don't you play a pretend-game about it? Pretend you can look inside of her and see one thing that's nice. What can you see in her that's nice? Everybody has a little bit of good in them, and you look until you find it. Then pretend that that one thing gets bigger and bigger until all of her is nice. Now change it into a believing game and say, 'Thank You, God, You are sending Your goodness into her and taking away all her bad feelings and helping her to be better.' "

So it happened that a week later Sally said, "Mother, I like that little girl in front of me now. She has a loving heart, that's what she has. And now I know the reason why she acts like that. It's because her mother doesn't take good care of her as you do of me, and her clothes aren't nice and she's afraid nobody will pay any attention to her. She does mean things to show off just so people will notice her. So I've decided to be her friend and now I am, and my, she's so nice to me! She thinks I'm just

74

wonderful. And the other kids are kinder to her now that she's got a friend."

So the believing game helped two little girls to be right-side-up and happy. In fact, it probably made the other girl's whole life a different kind of life. And really when you come to think of it, it made a schoolroom happier for everybody.

I am not telling you that everybody will change as soon as you think like this. There are some bigger and older people in the world who really want to be mean and it is very hard to change them. But lots of people do not really want to be bad at all, and when God's light comes into them they open up just as a flower opens up in the sun.

Do you think you could do in your schoolroom what Sally did in hers? It would be hard, I know. Any sissy can be mean, but it takes a brave person to be kind to someone whom other people don't like. But it is worth doing, even though it is hard. And if you will find someone who is lonely in school and learn to like that person, you will be surprised at how happy you will be.

Another way of learning to like people is to play that you are that person and to think, "How would I want the other kids to treat me?"

There was a little girl in school who could not go on the playground because the other children threw stones at her. She was not a bad child at all, and she was not stupid. In fact, her grades were higher than anybody's and perhaps that made the other children jealous. Or perhaps they just did not like her because her skin was darker than theirs and they had never taken time to get acquainted with her.

If those children had thought, "How would I like it if the other kids threw stones at me?" they would surely have stopped being mean right away. In fact, we would seldom be unkind to anyone if we stopped to think how we would feel in the other person's place.

BUNNY IN THE DRY LEAVES

Bunny in the dry leaves, rustle, rustle,
Bunny in the dry leaves, your little tail is white.
Bunny in the dry leaves, hustle, hustle!
Someone's coming—hurry up and scamper out of
    sight!

If I were just a bunny, hopping, hopping,
If I were just a bunny, and my little tail was
    white,
I wouldn't like a shotgun, popping, popping,
I wouldn't like for anyone to give me such a
    fright.

Chapter Eleven

❧⟫⟨❧

JESUS THE CARPENTER

Jesus was a carpenter,
    He sawed, as workmen do.
He hammered broken steps and things
    And made them good as new.

Did He ever dream of steps to heaven,
    The land from which He came
To live upon the lonely earth
    Where no one knew His name?

Did He ever play the nails were stars,
    The wood was heaven's floor
And He was making shining worlds
    As He had done before?

For He and God made everything—
  Stars and moon and sun—
While all the angels laughed with joy
  To see what had been done.

I'm glad He came on earth to live
  And tell us God is love
And so I thank Him every day,
  As angels do above.

I know of another way of learning to like
people, and that is to think about Jesus. He
loves us and wants to help us with everything,
but especially with forgiving—that is, learning
to like people. He is very good at that. He had
to be when He was on earth, for people were
not always nice to Him at all. Here He came,
out of God's great world of heaven where everyone is happy and good, in order to tell us that
God loves us and wants us to be happy and
good too. But although some people loved Him
very much, others did not understand Him. And
they were mad because He told them to be

kinder to others than they wanted to be. But He still loved them and asked God to forgive them because they did not know what they were doing. So He is very good at loving even the people who are mean, and if you ask Him to help you do it, He certainly can.

Then if you think, "But I just can't like that boy because he was terribly mean to me!" you can remember Jesus. People treated Him much worse than anyone has ever treated you. And He did not say that those bad people were good. But He asked God to make them good—and so can you, with Him to help you do it.

Now you may say, "But how can He help me do it, when He isn't here any more?"

But He is here, even though you can't see Him. If you wake in the night and you are frightened, don't you know it when your mother is in the house? You do not always go and climb into her bed, though sometimes when you are very frightened you may do so. Most of the time you just remember Mother and Dad asleep in their own room and you know

they are there even though you don't see them.
You can feel them right there. So you are com-
forted and go to sleep again.

Jesus is here now, in a way that is something
like that. And it is a very comforting way. If
we think about Him with loving thoughts, we
can feel Him here and we are happier. And if
we ask Him to help us, He can certainly do it.
He can help us in learning to like people and
He can help us in lots of ways.

A young man in the Air Force did this one

night. He was flying a plane and when he took off from the deck of the carrier, something went wrong. Instead of flying up to the sky, the plane dived down to the ocean. So this young man, whose nickname was Parson, knew that he was about to dive into the ocean and drown. So he said, "O Jesus, help me!"

And the very next second the plane turned its nose to the sky and up it went, into the starry night.

Parson looked down and saw searchlights playing over the ocean. So he radioed down to the carrier. "This is Parson," he said. "If you're looking for me, I'm up here."

When he landed safely on the carrier's deck, the commanding officer sent for him. "How did you *do* that?" he asked.

But Parson only touched his hat and said, "I don't know, Sir."

He knew that Jesus had helped him, but he did not like to say it. He felt like just keeping it a safe, happy secret inside of himself. I think it was all right for him to keep it a secret, and it is all right for us to do so. Because sometimes when we talk about things the power seems to go away from us, I don't know why.

But Parson smiled as he looked up at the sparkly sky, and inside of himself he said, "Thank You."

Chapter Twelve

→≫≫≪≪←

JUNIOR

Junior takes care of my memory room,
　　And a wonderful fellow is he,
For he keeps all my memories carefully stored
　　To help me be happy and free.

All I have known and all I have heard
　　Junior has sorted away.
He watches these memories all of the time
　　So I can forget them and play.

And if I am happy in taking a test
　　And trust him to find them for me ,
He'll look for them carefully, doing his best,
　　For he's friendly as friendly can be.

"Hunt for it, Junior," I'll say to him then,
    "It's somewhere down there in the files."
And up it will pop in the top of my mind
    While Junior inside of me smiles.

Of course the memories are not really in files
—big tin boxes such as Dad has in his office —
but I like to picture them that way for it helps
me understand the little inside mind that I call
Junior. I have told you something about the way
that he works. Now I want to tell you more
about him.

God has given him two big things to do for
us. One of them is to take care of the body, as
you know. How tiresome it would be if we had
to sit down after a meal and tell our stomachs
how to use the food that we have given them
—how to make it into blood and bone and
hair! It is very kind of God to give us this little
inside helper to take care of our bodies.

Junior's other task is to keep our memories
stored away and bring them to us when we
need them. Do you know that Junior keeps

everything that we have ever learned or known tucked away somewhere out of sight? I like to imagine Junior putting them away in files or big drawers, the important ones on top where we can easily find them and the ones that we care less about hidden away underneath. If we want to be sure to remember something, you know, we may help Junior by saying to him, "Now this is important," and by thinking about it quite a lot. After that, we can forget it and know that Junior is taking care of it. We do not have to remember all of our memories all the time, just as we do not have to think of our body machinery all the time.

When we go into a library we do not have to remember where all the books are kept. The librarian knows, and we can ask her. We ask the librarian nicely, because we trust her to take care of the books and we are polite to her.

But we are not very kind to our own unseen helper. We forget that he is timid and easily upset, and we are apt to frighten him. For instance, when we take a test in school we sometimes think, "Oh dear, I'm going to fail—I'm going to fail! I'll never remember all those things!" Then Junior hears the word "fail" and gets scared and confused. He doesn't know whether we want to remember or not and he doesn't know which drawer to look in first, and sometimes he just goes in the corner and sulks and won't help us. Then we can only remember those things that are on top of our minds.

Would you like to know a wonderful way of taking a test—one that will help you to do good work and help you to understand Junior too? All right, here it is. I have taught it to all kinds of people, from little girls who could not pass an arithmetic test to big men way over in England who were learning to be doctors and surgeons. And the little girls and the great men have told me that it works.

First of all, sit down and think about God just a minute and say, "Thank You, God, that everything I have learned is stored away in me. And thank You that You are going to help me with this test."

Then read the first question and answer it if you know it. If you cannot think of it right away, say to Junior, "You've got it down there in the files. Look it up for me like a good fellow while I go on and answer some other questions, and when you have found it, let me know. Thanks a lot."

After this, find a question or two that you do know, and answer them. Then come back to the first question and say to Junior, "All right? Have you found it?" And listen a while. Likely as not it will pop right up in your mind. But if it doesn't, just say, "Well, take a little more time if you like. I'll go on to another question and then come back, and by that time I'm sure you will have it."

By the time you come back to it, I will be very much surprised if Junior hasn't found it for you—that is, if you have ever studied the answer at all. Of course if you have not, there is nothing that Junior can do about it.

Now do you see what I mean about the mind

inside and how it works? It is like a younger brother or sister. It plays with you beautifully unless it gets frightened or upset, and if it does, it is no good at all.

So you see, if you try to keep in a good mood even when sick or when doing a hard thing like taking a test, then the little mind inside of you is much more likely to keep right on with its work. And if you talk nicely to it once in a while and say, "Oh, you're wonderful! You're doing a good job for me," then Junior is pleased and you can almost feel him smile. But if you are mad or scared or cross, he gets upset. And when he is upset or frightened, he cannot work for you.

MORE ABOUT JUNIOR

Junior's in the corner,
    He will not play today ,
He will not help me any more,
    No matter what I say.

"What's the matter, Junior?"
  Right away I know—
Junior heard me fuss and whine
  A little while ago.

He says, "You've got me so upset
  I simply cannot think!
If you will just be nice again,
  I'll help you in a wink."

Chapter Thirteen

→→→‹‹‹

THE WOODPECKER

Bird on the fir tree,
> *Thump, thump*

Bird on the fir tree,
> *Thump.*

Bird on the fir tree,
> *Peckety, peckety,*

Bird on the fir tree,
> *Thump.*

How do you know to go
> *Peckety, peckety?*

Who ever told you to
> *Thump?*

Catching your dinner by
                    Peckety, peckety,
Finding your supper by
                    Thump?

How does the woodpecker know where to find his food? And how does he know when winter is coming and he should go south? When he hunts food maybe he can smell the bugs in the tree, but he certainly can't smell winter coming! And even if he does know from the feeling in the air that winter is coming and all the bright flowers are going to die, how can he find his way a thousand miles to a country where the flowers never die? And how can he fly back to my fir tree when spring comes and all the daffodils toss their heads in the sun again?

But he does.

Here is a picture of birds looking at a sign saying, "Go south." One time in the mountains

I saw a sign to bears saying, "Do not eat food given to you by humans." But of course birds and bears do not really need signs nailed on a post, for they have a little sign inside of them.

One time I was in Arizona, a magic country where flowers like water lilies grow on top of prickly plants as big and round as barrels, and where there isn't any grass at all but only sand and sand. There isn't any grass, but the great tall mountains are made of red rocks and pink rocks and yellow rocks, and it is just as pretty as land covered with grass. And the prickly cactus plants gather up every bit of dew there is and hide it inside of their queer-looking stems. One of these plants is called a jumping cholla (only the people of Arizona say it like "choya"), because if you get too near to it the wind blows its thorns into you. While I was taking pictures of this strange plant I saw yellow orioles flying about. Then I saw a woodpecker on the great tall cactus that they call a saguaro (only they say it like "sahuaro"). It is a strange-looking thing, as tall as a church spire and as straight as a telephone pole. So I said to a friend, "Why, these birds are like my birds that live in my back yard two thousand miles away."

And my friend answered, "They are your birds. It is winter. Don't you know that in the wintertime your birds come here?"

But how could the woodpecker find his way back from that summer land to my fir tree? And how could the oriole swing again on the shiny birch outside my window? This is so strange that nobody really understands it. But they must have a little mind in them like the little inside mind in us that I call "Junior." Even if they do, that cannot explain how a young bird who has never been to Arizona knows to go there when winter is coming, and can find

the way to that sunny state. It seems as if God had put a little voice in the birds that tells them "Go south —winter is coming." People call this little voice "instinct," but that does not really explain it. Perhaps Jesus explained it better when He said that God watches over the birds.

Anyway, God has put a little voice inside of us too. People call it "conscience." But that does not explain it any more than the word "instinct" explains the little voice inside of the birds. Sometimes this voice inside of us does tell us what is right and what is wrong. And sometimes it tells us what is safe and what is not safe. It is as if the little mind inside of us knows more than we know ourselves. Sometimes it seems like Junior is telling us something, in the same way that Junior helps us remember. But it is more than that, because sometimes this voice inside warns us of dangers that Junior could not possibly know all by himself. Perhaps it is the voice of God that we hear, not with our ears but with our inside minds. Anyway, if we will learn to listen to this little voice, we will have happier and safer lives. Many grown people forget this and they say, "How can God let accidents happen to nice people?" And it isn't God's fault at all. He tries to tell all of us, but most of us are too far away from Him and we do not know how to listen to His voice as the birds do.

I know a young man who wanted to fly to an island in the Pacific Ocean, and he said, "Is that all right, God?" Then he sat quietly and listened, as we can learn to do. This young man had tried very hard to live close to God and to do what God wanted him to do. So he had learned to know it when God tried to speak to him. We do not always hear words inside of us —and neither do the birds. They just get a feeling. This man knew that when he got a queer, sad feeling about going somewhere, God was trying to tell him not to go. And he felt that queer, sad feeling about flying on Tuesday, so he did not do it. When he thought of going on Thursday and asked God about it he felt good, so he knew that it was all right to fly on Thursday and on Thursday he flew. And he got there all right. But on Tuesday a fog had come in from the sea and the plane had crashed and everybody on it was killed. Now you may say, why didn't God tell the other people not to fly on Tuesday? I am quite sure that He did, but they did not hear Him. They did not know how to be quiet and listen for that inside warning that is sometimes like a little voice and sometimes just a feeling. Or, perhaps, they were not keeping God's other laws like the law of love and so they were too far away from God to hear His voice. We have to be very near to God and learn how to open that door inside of us or else His voice cannot come in. And we must be sure that it really is His voice before we do what it says. Some grown people say things that are unkind or do things that are not nice and say, "God told me to do that." But God cannot tell us to do things that are bad. They must be listening to the voice of the badness that is in the world and not to God's voice.

So we must be careful. We may ask ourselves,

"Is that sensible?" And if it is not sensible but a silly idea like jumping off the roof, we may know that it is not God's voice. And we should ask ourselves, "Is that a good and kind thing to do?" And if we know that Mother would say it is naughty, then we may be sure it is not the voice of God. But how wonderful when it really is His voice and when He is telling us, "Do this or do that so that I can take care of you!"

So why don't you try listening to this inside voice? Just fold your hands and shut your eyes and listen to God. Sometimes you will seem to hear words inside of your mind, telling you ways of being more happy and more safe. Sometimes you will not hear words, but you will have a good feeling, as if God were smiling at you. And it will help you to do your work better and to have more fun when you play, and to be safer and happier all the time.

ORIOLE

Where will you go when the summer is dying?
Where will you go when the cold winds blow?
Straight on your course as an airplane flying
You will go south, by a path you know.

You will go south where the cactus towers,
Pillar of green in the shimmering sand,
With cholla that jumps and poinsettia flowers—
You will go south, to a summer land.

Chapter Fourteen

LITTLE DONKEY

Donkey, little donkey, you are acting like a mule!
Do not be so obstinate, and don't be such a fool!
No one wants to bother you and take your joy
away!
It's much more fun to work a bit than just to
run and play.

Think of what the world would be if no one
  worked at all!
No houses and no radio, no doll or bat or ball,
For work is really making things, and making
  things is fun,
So let's pretend our work is play, and work will
  soon be done.

Some children wish that they did not have to
work at all. They hang around the kitchen and
talk to Mother while she is doing the dishes
and never dry them nor put them away for her.
And if she says, "Come and help me with the
dishes," feeling very sad to see the children so
selfish, they say, "Well, I would, but I've got to
study now."

Then they go into the living-room and open
a book and look at the television. And after a
while they feel dull and unhappy and they don't
know why. But there is a very real reason why
they are not as happy as they could be. It is
because they really know that they should help
Mother and they will not do it. But Junior

knows they should be helping and when they don't it upsets him, so that he hides in a corner and will not help them. And after a while the television gets boring and these children get to fussing and fighting among themselves because they do not know what they want to do.

There is no use in just saying, "No, I won't work. I don't like to work. I won't listen to that voice." There is no use in saying it. Because we cannot stop the little mind inside of us from hearing it, and when Junior is unhappy then pretty soon we are completely up-side-down and nothing seems any fun.

Now I admit that too much work is tiresome, but a little work can be fun if we play it is a game.

Once when I was living beside a millpond in New Hampshire the neighbor's daughter came in and said, "Mother, may we go swimming? Because we want to wash the spinach."

I was surprised. "Wash the *spinach?*" I cried, as the little girl ran to get her bathing suit.

"For the freezer," the mother explained. "They

tow it out to the float in a big basket, then set it adrift, and pretend it is a school of fish and chase it in to the shore. By the time it gets there, it is clean."

Well, I should think it might be.

I doubt if you and I can wash the spinach in just this way. We do not have a millpond all our own. But we can often find some other way to make play of our work. We can pretend to be the old woman that lived in a shoe and the dishes can be our children, all washed and put into their right beds. Or the lawn-mower can be a big ship plowing over the rough waves of the

ocean. Or the vacuum cleaner can be a fierce dragon sucking the dirt out of the carpet. Or if we don't like to make up games like that, we

can just play a pretend-game of seeing Mother smiling and happy and rested so that she can read to us a while or play a game of checkers with us before we go to bed.

Of course we cannot make all of our work into fun, but that does not matter. It is good for us to do some work that is hard just as it is good for us to learn to keep God's laws even if it is hard to do. It keeps us from being sissies and it helps us to be strong. And besides, of course, it teaches us to do things and to make things. We really feel much better when we are doing things and making things than when we are just watching other people work. On days when we run about out-of-doors and think of nice games to play and help Dad mow the lawn or help Mother hang up her clothes, we are much happier than on days when we just sit still and look at the television for hours and hours. That is because God made us to be like Him and He does things and makes things all the time—He is a Creator. And after we have been doing things either in work or in play (and it is hard to tell the difference, because we sometimes work very hard in our play and we can learn to play very hard in our work), then we really feel good when we get through and sit down and rest. We have a lovely comfortable feeling because the little mind inside is pleased. And if we were to listen to God's voice, we would feel that He says, "That's good. I'm proud of you. Now you're keeping time with Me."

Perhaps your older brother plays in the school band and perhaps you have heard him practicing with somebody else on the big horn. If you have, then you know that when they keep time they make beautiful music. But when they don't keep time, it sounds just awful.

So when we are busy creating, we are keeping time with God and it is much easier for us to be right-side-up and happy.

THE DRUM

WHANG-doodle, WHANG-doodle, WHANG,
  whang, WHANG!
  BANG-doodle, BANG-doodle, BANG, bang,
  BANG!
The drum beats loud
  And the drum beats high
And the drum beats joy
  Right up to the sky!
The drum keeps time with the twirly thing
With the great big trumpets that shout and sing,
They all keep time
  As they march just so,
Follow the leader
  And away they go,
With a WHANG-doodle, WHANG-doodle,
  WHANG, whang, WHANG,
And a BANG-doodle,
      BANG-doodle,
        BANG, bang, BANG!

Chapter Fifteen

❧❧❧❦❦❦

ANGELS

Are there really angels
    With blue and purple wings?
Are there really seraphim
    And other shiny things?

The sky is full of a million stars
    With lots of other worlds
That whirl about them all the time
    As Mars and Venus whirl.

There's room for every sort of thing
    In God's big world out there,
For angels or for seraphim
    With shining, silver hair.

And wouldn't it be very odd
   If there could never be
A single angel anywhere
   But only folks like me.

Now I have told you lots of ways of being happy, and they are good ways. But of course we cannot be happy every minute while we are in this world, because many people do not know God's plans for happiness and so they act in a bad way. The more they act in a bad way the more badness they make in this world. Sometimes it makes sicknesses so bad that you and I and the doctor cannot heal them right now because we do not have enough power. One of these days we hope that lots and lots of people will try believing and then there will be much more of God's power on this earth. Maybe after a while there will be enough of it so that everything can be healed. Jesus said that some day that would be so. But in the meantime, we use the unhappy things in order to learn how to grow up and be strong, and in order to understand more about the laws of the outside world that God has made.

There really is a great big outside world, called the universe. It is made of stars that are bigger than our sun. They only look little because they are so far away. We don't know how many earths may swing around these stars nor what kinds of living things there may be upon those earths.

We read in our funny books about Superman and all kinds of fairytale people. I do not know anything about them. I think somebody just made up a story about them. But the Bible tells us about another world that it calls heaven, and about lovely, kind angels that live there, and great big angels called seraphim. And the Bible says that they come flying down here sometimes to watch over us and help us, and that we can ask them to help us even though we cannot see them.

I like to imagine them like the pictures on Christmas cards, with sweet faces and tall wings of blue and purple or of shining white. And sometimes I like to ask them to watch over me and see that I am safe. It does not matter whether they are exactly real or whether they are just something that we feel inside of our minds when we are safe and happy because God is near us. It makes me feel good to think about them just the same.

But I do know for sure that there is another world that we cannot see with our eyes, and that when we get through with this body and it is tired and worn out, we can shed it as a snake sheds its skin and go on to that other world that we call heaven. There is nothing to make us unhappy there, because no badness is allowed to come into that world. And it does not frighten me at all to think that some day I will go there, because Jesus who is my best friend is already there and He has everything ready for me. If you do not know about Jesus, I think you should read about Him in the Bible, because the story of His life is the most wonderful story in the world. He came to this earth out of God's heaven on purpose to help us. So we can trust Him to hold our hands and go with us when the time comes to go into that other world. Or if Grandmother or Grandfather has gone there, we do not need to be too sad, even though we miss them, because we know that they are living in a very happy way that we cannot understand.

One time I was flying in an airplane through a dark, dark night and looking at the black empty world below. Then we went over a city and it was as beautiful as a fairy-story thing, with all the lights twinkling and sparkling like diamonds. But they were so far away, and they looked so tiny and cold! And I thought, "If I didn't know what the earth is like, I would be frightened of landing there and getting out in that strange sparkling world."

But I did know what the earth is like. I knew that the lights were really homes, and that every home was warm and cozy inside and full of light, and I need not be afraid at all. Little children coming into them after playing hide-and-go-seek in the dark would find a mother there to cook their dinner and a father to watch over them and everything ready to make them happy.

Then I looked up into the sky of night and there were millions of other little lights twinkling, just like the lights of earth were twinkling. And I thought, "It isn't so different after all. There is another shining, starry world, and my grandmother and grandfather are there and my dear friend Jesus is there and the Father God is watching over all of us—it isn't so different after all."

NIGHT FLIGHT

Little stars of earth
    Far below, far below,
Little stars of earth
    Far below,
Heaven's stars are bright
Piercing through the night,
But oh, I love the sight
Of the little stars of earth
    Far below.

Every light is home,
      Far below, far below.
Every light is home
      Far below.
There is love and there is cheer,
Dinner ready, Mother near,
Never anything to fear,
In the little lights of home
      Far below.

Are the stars on high
      Little homes, little homes?
Are the stars on high
      Little homes?
Full of radiance bright and clear,
Happy angels, Father near,
Never anything to fear
In the stars that shine on high—
      The Father's homes.